entrusted

A Study of 2 Timothy

BETH MOORE

Leader Guide

LifeWay Press®
Nashville, Tennessee

Published by LifeWay Press®. © 2016 Beth Moore

ISBN 978-1-4300-5502-0 • Item 006103966

Dewey Decimal Classification: 248.84
Subject Headings: FAITH \ DISCIPLESHIP \ WITNESSING

Unless otherwise noted, all Scripture quotations are taken from the Holman Christian Standard Bible®, Copyright © 1999, 2000, 2002, 2003, 2009 by Holman Bible Publishers. Used by permission. Holman Christian Standard Bible®, Holman CSB®, and HCSB® are federally registered trademarks of Holman Bible Publishers.

To order additional copies of this resource, write to LifeWay Church Resources Customer Service; One LifeWay Plaza; Nashville, TN 37234-0113; fax 615.251.5933; phone toll free 800.458.2772; email *customerservice@lifeway.com*; order online at *www.lifeway.com*; or visit the LifeWay Christian Store serving you.

Printed in the United States of America

Adult Ministry Publishing, LifeWay Church Resources, One LifeWay Plaza, Nashville, TN 37234-0152

About the Author

CYNTHIA HOPKINS speaks at women's and youth events and writes articles, curriculum, and devotions for a wide variety of LifeWay publications, including a monthly column in *Parenting Teens* magazine. Her devotional book, *What Now?*, helps equip teenagers to live out their faith after the spiritual high of a camp or retreat experience. Cynthia is the founder of Platform 320, a nonprofit ministry that encourages women to step up to the lives they were made for.

Cynthia is married to Clay, who is the Associate Pastor at FBC College Station, TX. They have two children: Brandon, a senior at Texas A&M University, and Abby, a senior in high school.

Check out Cynthia's blog at *www.cynthiahopkins.org*.

CONTENTS

Introduction .... page 4

12 Signs You're a Fantastic Facilitator.. page 5

Mentoring Matters.. page 6

Optional Group Study Formats... page 8

(coed groups, neighborhood studies, large group, small group, retreats)

Five Levels of Participation... page 10

Session 1.. page 12

Session 2.. page 14

Session 3.. page 16

Session 4.. page 18

Session 5.. page 20

Session 6.. page 22

Viewer Guide Answers .... page 24

Cue the Confetti! .... page 25

Introduction

Timothy likely had a roomful of people representing various life experiences and difficulties looking to him for leadership. The believers in Ephesus had questions about the Scriptures and wanted to know how to live them out when they were facing intense struggles of circumstance, persecution, and warfare. He couldn't have been able to relate to all of them. He felt ill-equipped to lead. And without his spiritual father, Paul, close by, he probably worried he would fail them all.

Can you relate?

You have been entrusted, too. As Paul meant his letter to exhort and encourage Timothy, let this study be for you. Turn each page first not as one teaching others, but as one being taught.

The intent of this leader guide is to help you facilitate discussion and to promote a connection among participants that will far outlast the six sessions of study. It is not meant to be a script. Rather, it is filled with suggestions to help you discover the best way to approach discussion in your particular group.

Here is a suggested outline:

- Prep your material/supplies.
- Welcome/Icebreaker.
- Review homework from previous week.
- Watch video session.
- Discuss.
- Prayer.
- Follow up.

12 Signs You're a Fantastic Facilitator

You might not be the type of person who thinks about gathering extra pens for the Bible study group you're leading; on the rare occasion you do remember, absolutely zero of them have a daisy hot glued to the end. The email/phone list you collect at the first meeting might be written on a napkin because that is the only paper product available at the last minute when the thought occurs to you to gather that information. You might even make it through the entire study without once bringing a tray of brownies.

And here's the beauty of it all: God will use you anyway.

Your effectiveness as a Bible study leader has far less to do with experience, personality, and delicious desserts than willingness, authenticity, and a teachable spirit. There are some steps you can take, though, to provide an environment conducive to great discussion and growth. Here are 12 signs you're taking those steps and effectively leading your Bible study group.

1. **YOU KNOW YOUR ROLE.** Ultimately, the Holy Spirit facilitates every bit of growth and learning that takes place. You're simply the conduit He uses to get that growing out in the open. Let that truth take a load off!

2. **YOU THINK OUTSIDE THE BOX.** There's a learning curve to figuring out what works and what doesn't with each group; good leaders embrace it and are flexible.

3. **YOU LOOK FOR THE BALANCE BETWEEN GUILT AND "IT DOESN'T MATTER."** Group members tend to stop showing up when they get behind on homework, typically somewhere around week 3. Your approach can do a lot toward maintaining strong attendance and helping women stick to it. Asking, "What do you think?" instead of "What did you write?" is a good place to start.

4. **YOU TRUST THE GROUP.** Encourage members to highlight meaningful truths from their homework and be prepared to share them in class. Then let their thoughts and questions help facilitate discussion.

5. **YOU ASK YOUR OWN QUESTIONS.** This book is simply a source of ideas. As you study, add to the ideas you find here by jotting down your own thoughts and questions. Then use those as you lead the group.

6. **YOU ASK QUESTIONS THAT PROMPT DISCUSSION.** Should you ask open-ended questions? Yes.

7. **YOU ASK YOURSELF THE QUESTIONS YOU PLAN TO ASK THE GROUP.** If you find a question awkward or difficult to answer, they probably will, too.

8. **YOU LOOK TO EXPLORE WHAT PEOPLE ARE LEARNING MORE THAN WHAT THEY ALREADY KNOW.** Here's what makes people feel like they don't belong—when they come

into a class and everyone seems to know all the answers. Everyone doesn't know all the answers, but the discussion sometimes makes it seem that way. To some extent, we should all struggle with the truth every time we study the Scriptures. The direction of the questions you ask can help with that.

9. **YOU EMBRACE SILENCE.** Sometimes people need to let a question marinate a bit before they answer. Resist the urge to rush the process. Rather than answering it yourself or jumping to another question, don't be afraid to embrace a moment or two of silence.

10. **YOU INVEST IN PEOPLE.** Anyone can push a button on a remote. There's more to it than that, and that's why there likely wasn't a long list of volunteers playing rock-paper-scissors to see who got to facilitate this semester's study.

11. **YOU'RE AUTHENTIC.** Don't ask any question of your group you're not willing to answer yourself. In fact, you should be ready to answer them on occasion when you need to get the discussion started.

12. **YOU PRAY BOLDLY AND PRAY BIG.** In the first video session, Beth points out, "We don't just study the Scriptures to build up Bible knowledge. We get to know the Scriptures to be equipped to do what He's called us to do." Pray it happens in your group. Pray it happens in you.

Mentoring Matters

Mentor: noun—a trusted counselor or guide

The Letter of 2 Timothy illuminates the benefit of mentoring, which is a major theme of the *Entrusted* study. Through it, we will discover …

MENTORING MAKES US MORE EFFECTIVE. In Session One, Beth notes, "A vital part of our effectiveness is our connectedness." We cannot develop our gifts without connectedness to the body of Christ. We need each other.

MENTORING IS A NECESSARY RISK. It accepts and receives the hard questions. In Session Two, we learn, "If we can't stand to be questioned, we will be too childish to stand guard."

MENTORING NATURALLY TAKES PLACE IN THE BODY OF CHRIST. In Session Three, we're encouraged not to force mentoring relationships but to let them happen naturally within the context of our connectedness to the church.

MENTORING IS A KEY WEAPON FOR THE BATTLE. In Session Four, Beth exhorts from 1 Timothy 6:12, "This faith-life is a fight from beginning to end," and "If you are not fighting, you are being defeated, or you are of no use to the gospel."

MENTORING STRENGTHENS US. In Session Five, we learn we either weaken or build up each others' spiritual muscles.

MENTORING POINTS TO THE GREATER REALITY. Beth notes in Session Six that Paul was inspired to encourage us about our future lives.

MENTORING IS NOT MEANT TO BE A PROGRAM OR A PASSING FAD. It is a vital part of the growth of the church through the ages, and it's happening right now in your Bible study. That's one reason we get together to discuss what God has taught us during the week—so we can be encouraged and challenged by what God is doing in one another.

But what about after the study? Mentoring is vital, but still often overlooked as an ongoing necessity of life in the body of Christ. Here are some ways you can use *Entrusted* as a springboard for deep and continuing relationships, even after the study ends.

- **Pair Bible study members**—an older with a younger, if possible. You can do this on day one with two purposes in mind: to encourage accountability during the study and to foster ongoing mentoring relationships.

- **Encourage pairs to meet weekly, biweekly, or monthly.** We can get together for the purpose of spiritual growth without it being an event listed on the church calendar. Call it lunch, call it catching up, call it an afternoon at the park—it doesn't matter what it looks like, as long as we're recognizing the priority of doing life together and investing in other believers.

- **Exchange phone numbers.** Paul continued to mentor Timothy even when they could no longer meet face to face. Mentoring can still happen among those whose lives are busy and full.

- **As a group, compile a list of good books, Bible studies, and blogs.** Print the list and give to group members as the study ends. Encourage them to use the list as a resource of potential study or discussion in mentoring relationships going forward.

- **Pray with intention.** Rather than praying together as a whole group each week in opening or in closing, consider breaking into small groups of two or three on occasion. This will help foster the formation of relationships within the group that will last beyond the study.

- **Encourage the asking of good questions.** Create a short list of questions mentors can ask mentees as they seek to form deeper relationships for the purpose of spiritual growth. Print these or write your own: What are you reading and studying in addition to your quiet time that is deepening your relationship with God? What is God teaching you right now? Do you feel like you're wrestling with God in any area of life right now? How are you handling that? Have you stepped out in faith lately? Who have you had an opportunity to share the gospel with?

Optional Study Formats

COED GROUPS

If your study includes both male and female participants, consider breaking into gender-specific small groups for discussion each week. If you don't break into smaller groups or this is not possible, be intentional about including everyone by considering the male perspective as you prepare your questions. Be encouraged that 2 Timothy, the *Entrusted* viewing guides, and homework pages apply entirely to both men and women.

NEIGHBORHOOD STUDY

This particular study is primarily directed toward believers; however, you can still use it as a way to reach out to your neighbors, opening discussion about the gospel message and what it means to follow Christ. Choose a day of the week and time to meet, then invite your neighbors to your home for small group study. As you ask questions in this context, be reminded that even unbelievers want to be effective in what they feel is their purpose in the world. Lead participants to see that ultimately, this is dependent upon relationship with Christ and connection to His body, the church.

LARGE GROUP

If you expect a large number of participants, enlist additional leaders for smaller groups of 12-15 each or a size that meets the needs of your group. Begin each session in the large group with a time of welcome and watching the video session. You might also include a time of worship through singing. Then break into small groups, where leaders facilitate discussion of the video message and previous week's study.

SMALL GROUP

Since you're staying together as one group throughout the session, this format offers the most flexibility. Choose to discuss homework first, then watch and discuss the video. Or, after a welcome and icebreaker question, show the video then discuss the homework and teaching session together.

RETREAT

Frame your retreat sessions around the six video sessions of *Entrusted*. Consider planning your retreat according to this schedule, using times appropriate with the group, location, etc.:

Friday Evening:

1. Dinner. Assign a small group leader to each table. Offer ice-breaker questions to help groups begin to connect.

2. Worship. Pre-enlist a worship leader to lead your group in a few songs.

3. View Session One DVD.

4. Small group discussion. Depending on your setting, lead groups to discuss at tables or to move to other pre-determined locations. Use the questions found on pp. 12-13 of this book to lead discussion.

5. Break. Options: free time, mixer, or activities that fit your group.

6. Worship.

7. View Session Two DVD.

8. Small group discussion.

Continue this format throughout the day on Saturday, or through the length of your retreat. Be sure to include ample time in between sessions for meals and opportunities to connect and reflect. End your retreat with a closing challenge and time of large group worship.

Five Levels of Participation

1. WATCH VIDEOS
2. COMPLETE HOMEWORK
3. HANDWRITE 2 TIMOTHY
4. READ ARTICLES
5. MEMORIZE 2 TIMOTHY

LEVEL 1: Participate in the video sessions

Through the years people drop out of Bible study because they couldn't keep up with the homework. Don't think for a moment that if you can't do all of it, you're better off doing none of it. A shorter time in Scripture is far better than none at all. Watch the video sessions even if you can't get your homework assignments accomplished.

LEVEL 2: Participate in the video sessions
+ do the weekly homework assignments

Moving up to level 2 in which you meet with God on the pages of Scripture numerous times each week exponentially increases your experience. When you turn the last page, you will truly know 2 Timothy and the important circumstances surrounding Paul's final letter. If you've got the stamina to do the homework (and you do!), you've got it in you to view the sessions. Keep in mind that many of the larger themes are addressed in the sessions, so try your hardest to view the coinciding ones at the end of each week of homework.

LEVEL 3: Participate in the video sessions
+ do the weekly homework assignments
+ handwrite 2 Timothy

Each time we come to a new segment of the letter, Beth will ask you to read it then handwrite it in the back of the Bible study book on the pages designed for this exercise (or in a notebook or journal). If you don't choose level 3, you'll simply read the portion. This option is simply available for those who want to take the next step to retain what they're learning.

LEVEL 4: Participate in the video sessions
        + do the weekly homework assignments
        + handwrite 2 Timothy
        + read "Next Level with Melissa"

Many people have asked how they could go even deeper in the material. Melissa brings a more academic approach to some of the concepts each week.

LEVEL 5: Participate in the video sessions
        + do the weekly homework assignments
        + handwrite 2 Timothy
        + read "Next Level with Melissa"
        + memorize 2 Timothy

You'll find a short tutorial on the *Entrusted* website (*lifeway.com/entrusted*) and in the DVD bonus material that may help you if you're interested in this level.

Needless to say, we're not recommending trying to memorize all of 2 Timothy in the five short weeks of this series. The best recommendation for setting your pace is whatever works. Not one second you spend on Scripture memory is ever wasted. Think about doing it! Pray about it! Then, some of you, do it!

Okay, friend, which level seems the most doable for you right now?

1   2   3   4   5

PROMOTING THE STUDY

Let us do the hard part! We've designed free promotional tools like bulletin inserts, posters, invitation cards, PowerPoint slides, short teaching clips, promotional videos, and social media for you to announce your upcoming *Entrusted* study to your church and community. Find these tools at *lifeway.com/entrusted*.

Session One

BEFORE THE SESSION

Enlist small group leaders and meet prior to Session One to give a brief overview of the study, offer tips for facilitating discussion, emphasize how to build mentoring relationships, and explain the weekly format from page 4 of this book. Plan especially for Week One, readying leaders to come early to distribute materials and welcome participants as they arrive. Pray together for each other and for group members.

Provide name tags, Bible study books, Bibles, pens, and pencils as needed.

DURING THE SMALL GROUP SESSION

Welcome participants. Begin compiling a group list where each member can record his or her name, phone number, and email address.

Icebreaker: Lead participants to share their names and why they came. Ask: What have you heard or studied in the past about Paul and Timothy? What do you know about 2 Timothy?

Take a moment to explain why you and/or your team chose this particular study and what you're praying God does in your group through it. Direct the group to take a few moments to pray in smaller groups of 3-4 that God will use these six weeks to do a work in the life of each participant for the glory of His great name.

View the Session One video.

Call attention again to points 1 and 2 on the Session One viewer guide.

DISCUSSION QUESTIONS

· What might keep a person in this room from believing "mighty servant turned loose" and "effectiveness" for God's kingdom purposes would ever describe her?
· In response to those hang-ups, which point—3, 4, or 5—speaks to you the most right now? Invite learners to share any other truths that stood out to them during the video session.
· How are you challenged by the enormous goal in this Bible study?
· Considering how God has spoken to you already in Session One. How can this group pray for you?

Lead the group in prayer.

Encourage participants to continue the study this week by completing the assigned homework pages. Take a few minutes to scan the first week's daily assignments together. Explain the design of *Entrusted* is for members to complete a week of study prior to each weekly meeting. Before the next meeting, complete Week One. Note they can expect each daily assignment to take approximately 30-45 minutes. Encourage members to highlight or make note of questions or statements that particularly stand out to them as they complete the daily assignments and to note any questions they may have.

Thank members for coming, and tell them to look for an email from you during the week. Dismiss the group.

AFTER THE SESSION

Compile all registration cards or lists, and if you have a large group of participants, divide among small group leaders.

MIDWEEK MESSAGE: A few days after your first meeting, email or text a thought or question from Day Three along with encouragement to finish the week's homework. Consider also pairing members to serve as homework encouragement partners.

Create attendance sheets for each group leader.

MY PLAN: SESSION ONE

PERSONALIZE IT! Outline your own agenda and questions for leading Session One. Review the homework and discussion questions that would resonate the most with your group.

Session Two

BEFORE THE SESSION

Complete Week One in the Bible study book.

Pray for group members.

Touch base with small group leaders to see if they have any needs for the upcoming meeting.

DURING THE SMALL GROUP SESSION

Greet members and welcome new participants. Add to the group list names, phone numbers, and email addresses of anyone new.

Icebreaker: Name one thing you know God has entrusted to you. What steps do you presently take to grow in effectiveness in that area?

Pray God will use today's study and discussion to deepen each participant's understanding of how God has entrusted and emboldened her to respond to Him in trustworthiness.

Review the week's Discussion Questions. Refer to pages 5-6, "12 Signs You're an Effective Facilitator" in this leader guide for tips on how to best engage participants in discussion.

REVIEW

- What stood out to in your study this week? Was anything particularly challenging to you? How so?
- Review the activity on the biographical information of Saul (p. 18). What did you learn new from completing this assignment?
- Check the map on the inside back cover of the Bible study book and record which directions Barnabas and Paul went. How did the gospel multiply through their division?
- What new truths did you learn about Timothy during this week's homework?
- Refer to the key activity on page 43. Discuss your answers with your group.
- What are you hoping to learn or do going forward?

View the Session Two video

Call attention again to the exhortation Beth gave that sums up the entire six-week course: *Guard the trust*. Recall what the trust entails (the gospel and the gifting) and discuss the first point.

DISCUSSION QUESTIONS

· Who is a person you know who highly esteems the gospel?
· What could be the consequences of not respecting and valuing the gifts God has given you?
· What would it look like this week for you to highly and favorably value the gospel through your attitudes and actions?
· What does it look like when you honor God with your gifts?
· How can this group pray for you?

Lead the group in prayer.

Encourage participants to continue the study this week by responding to the truths the Holy Spirit has impressed upon them and by completing the assigned homework pages. Remind them of Beth's question: "What have you got going on in your life that is better than Jesus?"

Thank members for coming, and tell them to look for an email from you again this week. Dismiss the group.

AFTER THE SESSION

Touch base with small group leaders to address suggestions, problems, or needs.

Midweek Message: Sometime during the week, email or text this question from the Session Two video: "When all is said and done, could we be trusted with what was entrusted to us?" Add the text of a brief prayer you're praying for participants this week, such as, "Father, continue to speak to (name) as she digs further into Your Word this week. Fill her with the highest esteem for the gospel and the gifts You have given her, that she might go forth for the glory of Your great name in this world."

MY PLAN: SESSION TWO

Personalize it! Outline your own agenda and questions for leading Session Two. Review the homework and discussion questions that would resonate the most with your group.

Session Three

BEFORE THE SESSION

Complete Week Two in the Bible study book.

Pray for group members.

Touch base with small group leaders to see what they need for the upcoming session.

DURING THE SMALL GROUP SESSION

Begin by sharing a brief story about a mentoring-type relationship you have had and what that relationship means/meant to you.

Icebreaker: People can mentor one another in a variety of ways. We may have spiritual mentors, work mentors, or other types of mentors to help us learn and grow. Remember, mentoring can be formal or informal. Name someone who has mentored you and one way that relationship has influenced your life.

Pray, thanking God for the privilege of meeting together with others in the body of Christ to encourage and exhort one another, and to do life together. Ask Him to use the discussion and video message to ignite spiritual fervor among you.

REVIEW

· Day Two looks at the relationship between Paul and Timothy. What are some ways their relationship might be more impressive than the traditional parent/child paradigm (p. 57)?
· Review the two G-words in Day Four (p. 66). God has entrusted us with the gospel of Jesus Christ and the Holy Spirit-gifting to share it. How does that truth transform how you live each day?
· Page 76 refers to Spiritual Refreshers. What did you learn and receive from these verses?
· How did this week's study cause you to think or act differently?

View the Session Three video.

Invite participants to respond to Beth's statement, "We were made for fire." Point out we all experience times in our lives when that fire begins to die down. Recall the things Beth said has worked for her to reignite spiritual fervor: try different things, get trained, Scripture, prayer, music, exposing self to people who are a lot of fire.

DISCUSSION QUESTIONS

· What do you do to reignite spiritual fervor? Why do we sometimes do nothing?
· What is your greatest challenge to being "on fire" for God? How can you combat this challenge?
· You've got to have God to serve God. What are the ways you can be more intentional in your relationship with God so you are equipped to serve Him?
· Compare and contrast what a spirit of fear produces as it perverts power, love, and self-control.
· How can this group pray for you?

Encourage participants to continue the study this week by completing the assigned homework pages as a way of fanning into flame the gift of God. Pray 2 Timothy 1:6-7 over the group.

Thank members for coming, and tell them to look for an email from you again this week. Dismiss.

AFTER THE SESSION

Touch base with small group leaders to address suggestions, problems, or needs.

Midweek Message: Late this week, email or text group members one of the personal questions listed in the homework pages. Share your response to the question and encourage members to text or email their response to their homework encouragement partner or another group member.

MY PLAN: SESSION THREE

Personalize it! Outline your own agenda and questions for leading Session Three. Review the homework and discussion questions that would resonate the most with your group.

Session Four

BEFORE THE SESSION

Complete Week Three in the Bible study book.

Pray for group members.

Touch base with small group leaders to equip them for the upcoming session.

DURING THE SMALL GROUP SESSION

Welcome the group and share prayer requests. Pray for the needs that were mentioned. Thank God for His Word, His Spirit, and the community of believers, all of which serve to make us aware of truth and evil. Invite Him to use today's discussion and teaching to give us clarity about the fight we are in as we walk this earth.

Icebreaker: If you had to choose one, would you say you feel empowered or entangled? Why? Knowing what you know already about Paul's letter to Timothy, in what ways might Timothy have felt entangled? Empowered?

REVIEW

- Was there something you read that you long to relate to in your spiritual life, but can't seem to get there? Explain.
- Review the activity on 2 Timothy 2:2 comparing additional verses that infer the gospel process (p. 83). Discuss your answers with your group.
- Day Three challenged us to look for God-approval (p. 93). When was the last time you tasted how toxic the desire for human approval and affirmation could be? Explain.
- Discuss the house illustration activity on page 99.
- How do you deal with controversy and opposition? (Look at Paul's strategy on p. 105 to help with the discussion.)
- Besides dealing with your own stuff, how has this week's study encouraged or challenged you in relationships with others and their stuff (Elicit general responses; no names)?

View the Session Four video.

Share something from today's teaching that was especially meaningful to you.

DISCUSSION QUESTIONS

· Of the points on your listening guide, which stands out the most to you? Why?
· How were you challenged when you heard that you are not your own worst enemy, but your enemy's best accomplice?
· How have you seen yourself (or others) have a sincere and pure devotion to Christ, yet be completely seduced by the devil?
· Do you believe that God is continually and mercifully after our good? Why or why not?
· How has Jesus been the best part of the ups and downs in your life?

Encourage participants to continue the study this week by completing the assigned homework pages as a way of fighting the good fight. Pray, thanking God that "even amid the evil that beleaguers or befalls us," He is "continually and mercifully after our good." Invite Him to draw all of you into deeper dialogue and dependency upon Him this week.

Thank members for coming, and tell them to look for an email from you again this week. Dismiss.

AFTER THE SESSION

Touch base with small group leaders to address suggestions, problems, or needs.

Midweek Message: Early this week, email or text group members this message: Jesus is the best part! Philippians 3:7-8, "But everything that was a gain to me, I have considered to be a loss because of Christ. More than that, I also consider everything to be a loss in view of the surpassing value of knowing Christ Jesus my Lord. Because of Him I have suffered the loss of all things and consider them filth, so that I may gain Christ."

MY PLAN: SESSION FOUR

Personalize it! Outline your own agenda and questions for leading Session Four. Review the homework and discussion questions that would resonate the most with your group.

Session Five

BEFORE THE SESSION

Complete Week Four in the Bible study book.

Pray for group members.

Touch base with small group leaders to see if they need anything for the upcoming session.

DURING THE SMALL GROUP SESSION

Welcome the group and congratulate them for making it this far!

Icebreaker: How do you see people doing the hard work of the church on a weekly basis? Today's video is about servants of God doing the work of ministry. There is an Irish proverb that says, "Nodding the head does not row the boat." What does that mean to you, specifically in what God is teaching you in this study?

Pray and invite God today to continue the work in each of you He started through this study.

REVIEW

- If you were telling someone not involved in this study one thing God taught you in *Entrusted* this week, what would it be?
- Is there a question or statement you read in *Entrusted* this week that you'd like to dig into further? If so, explain.
- How might the things you are learning in Bible study apply to your church and serving the Lord in your church?
- Day Three looked at the tension between the strong-willed and the weak-willed (pp. 128-129). How would you describe yourself and those leaning upon your spiritual maturity?
- How have you allowed the giftedness and serving lives of others to distract you from what you have to give (p. 133)?

View the Session Five video.

DISCUSSION QUESTIONS:

· Of the five points about rowers on your listening guide, which is most difficult for you currently? Why?
· Which of the five points require mentoring-type relationships?
· How would you explain the example of the rowers to a new Christian as you encourage that person to serve God?
· Name one practical way you can put one of these points into practice this week.

Encourage participants to finish strong this week by completing the assigned homework pages. Pray, thanking God for the camaraderie He gives His servants on earth. Ask Him to fill each participant with the resolve and courage this week to row well.

Thank members for coming and encourage them to approach this last week of study with joyful expectation. Remind them to look for an email or text from you again this week. Dismiss.

AFTER THE SESSION

Touch base with small group leaders to address suggestions, problems, or needs.

Midweek Message: After a day or two has passed, email or text group members a question from day four or five with a note, "Here's what's coming later this week! Finish strong, and see you soon for our final session of *Entrusted*."

MY PLAN: SESSION FIVE

Personalize it! Outline your own agenda and questions for leading Session Five. Review the homework and discussion questions that would resonate the most with your group.

Session Six

BEFORE THE SESSION

Complete Week Five in the Bible study book.

Pray for group members.

Touch base with small group leaders to see if they have any needs for the upcoming session.

DURING THE SMALL GROUP SESSION

Welcome the group to the final session of *Entrusted*. Pray, thanking God for His Word that speaks to us today as powerfully as it spoke to its original readers so long ago. Ask Him to bless the teaching and group discussion today in bigger ways than you even know to think or ask.

Icebreaker: Up to this point in your life, what have been some of your expectations of God? Do you have expectations of God for your future? Why or why not? What are they?

REVIEW

· How would you say you have grown in the area of personal Bible study during this study?
· What will you do next to continue your relationship with God through His Word? Who will partner with you in that?
· In Day One of your homework (p. 150), you looked at the tension between being urgent with the gospel and patient with people. Which do you find more challenging and why?
· Day Four looked at a number of people who crossed paths with Paul and Timothy. What did you learn by studying these relationships this week?
· Day Five discussed the final verses of Paul's letter to Timothy, 2 Timothy 4:16-22 (p. 173). What stood out most to you and why?

View the Session Six video.

DISCUSSION QUESTIONS

· As you conclude this study, what will help you remember that your labor in ministry for God's kingdom is not in vain?
· How does Paul's eternal focus help you fine tune your expectations of reward from the Father?
· In what situation of life do you most need to remember these encouragements Paul gave to Timothy?
· How can this group pray for you going forward?

Pray, thanking God for the abiding truth that none of our labor on this earth will ever be in vain. Ask Him to continue teaching and leading participants to thrive in their daily lives and service for Him.

Thank members for joining you in *Entrusted*. Enjoy a time of celebration with your group.

AFTER THE SESSION

Meet with small group leaders to evaluate and discuss any plans for follow up.

Midweek Message: Sometime this week, email or text group members a word of thanks for their willingness to connect with others in Christian community through Bible study. Attach a list of good books, Bible studies, and blogs as described in Mentoring Matters on page 6, encouraging group members to continue investing in one another and deepening relationships.

MY PLAN: SESSION SIX

Personalize it! Outline your own agenda and questions for leading Session Six. Review the homework and discussion questions that would resonate the most with your group.

Viewer Guide Answers

SESSION 1

1. Mighty Servants; turned loose; this globe; great name; Jesus

2. ramp up our effectiveness; Christ's; Your; Our; connectedness; His great glory

3. whole new level; takes faith; willing; believe; dramatically change; true; since birth

4. erroneous estimations; our serving lives; who adore; quickly abhor

5. Just keep getting back up

SESSION 2

Pastoral Epistles: 1 Timothy, 2 Timothy, Titus

1. effectively guard; don't highly esteem; another person's treasured possession; safe; as it was

2. can't stand; be questioned; too childish; stand guard; character; expected; entitled; addictive

3. is not; eagerness; take charge; to take the charge

SESSION 3

fire; again; supernatural unction; fulfill divine purpose; our earthly tenure; have; serve; the gifts for ministry; publicly recognized; validation; public; private letter; cowardice; perversions; three opposing; powerlessness; abuse; lust; hate; drive; control others; achieving power; able; capable; accomplishment; self-discipline; sound mind; sound judgment; sound mind

SESSION 4

called

1. forces of evil; meaner; abler; ever pictured; entangled; entrusted; not your own worst enemy; own worst enemy's; accomplice; sincere; pure; completely seduced

2. faith-life; fight; beginning to end; fight; conflict; contend for victory; take pains; award contest; nerve; uttermost; goal; good; beautiful

3. evil; beleaguers; befalls us; mercifully; our good

4. set up the system; demands dialogue; dependency; function properly

5. Jesus is the best part

SESSION 5

under; rower; common sailor

1. Rowers; build up; rowing downstream

2. rhythm; sync; team; concentrated effort

3. Rowing; amount of repetition

4. Rowers; other's backs

SESSION 6

1. unapologetic expectancy; reward

2. direct interaction; Christ

3. exceedingly vivacious existence; kingdom

4. heavenly; translucent

5. see that face; fully know; he'd been known

6. must know to thrive; one ounce; labor; ever be in vain

CUE THE CONFETTI!

You've done an amazing job leading your group through the *Entrusted* Bible Study! If you enjoyed studying God's Word with Beth Moore together, you'll love the experience of LIVE Bible study at a Living Proof event near you or via simulcast. So gather your girlfriends and get a Living Proof Beth Moore event on your calendar today!

Visit **lifeway.com/livingproof**
for dates, locations, and details.

LifeWay Women | events

EVERYTHING IS BETTER WHEN SHARED

Women love to share good things with each other. We love to tell our friends when we get a great deal, find a new bakery in town, listen to an interesting podcast, or discover a life-saving parenting tip—we'll share anything that helps a sister in Christ continue on in her journey. So, why not share a powerful women's conference experience with your friends or church group? It's easy. Anyone with a willing heart can be a group leader. If you're already the one who makes things happen, sends the emails, and gathers your friends, this will be a breeze.

You've experienced the impact that the truth of God's Word can have. And you know that something special happens when we pull away from our everyday surroundings and give ourselves room to breathe. There are hurting women all around you, desperate for hope and peace. Help these women find that breathing room by giving them this opportunity.

TRY THESE TIPS WHEN BRINGING A GROUP TO AN EVENT:

- Decide on an event location and date.
- Gather names of those you want to join you.
- Secure hotel rooms and transportation.
- Make sure everyone has registered for the event.
- Organize a meeting place and time to depart, and set up other necessary meet-up times and locations.

- Collect cell phone numbers for everyone in your group.
- Think through weather conditions and meal options.
- Plan a couple of activities for the drive home to help the ladies share their experiences.
- Schedule a Bible study after the event to keep women connected.

Find all the information you need to get started, including how to contact the event concierge for your city, at **lifeway.com/livingproof**

LIVING PROOF *live*

with **Beth Moore**

The ultimate live Bible study event.

Experience Living Proof Live with your study group!

lifeway.com/livingproof

LifeWay Women | events

Bring Beth to your church!

5 Reasons You Can't Pass This Up!

1. It's convenient.
Give busy women a chance to attend this one-day event without traveling far.

2. It makes for the perfect women's retreat.
Invest in the women at your church by providing a day of life-changing teaching.

WELCOME

3. It builds relationships.
Hold an event where women from all over the community can meet and worship together.

4. It's flexible.
Choose a date that works best for your church with access to the simulcast up to 30 days after the event airs.

5. It's hassle free.
Plan an effortless event with access to a personal concierge who will help walk you through planning, promotion, and technical questions.

Register your church at
lifeway.com/lpsimulcast

LIVING PROOF simulcast

LifeWay Women | events

"You and I are in this together, so come along and let's get this journey off the ground."

– Beth Moore

Experience Living Proof Live
lifeway.com/livingproof

LifeWay Women | events

THE BUSY WOMAN'S GUIDE TO BETH MOORE BIBLE STUDIES

If you enjoyed studying *Entrusted* with Beth, you'll love her other Bible studies.

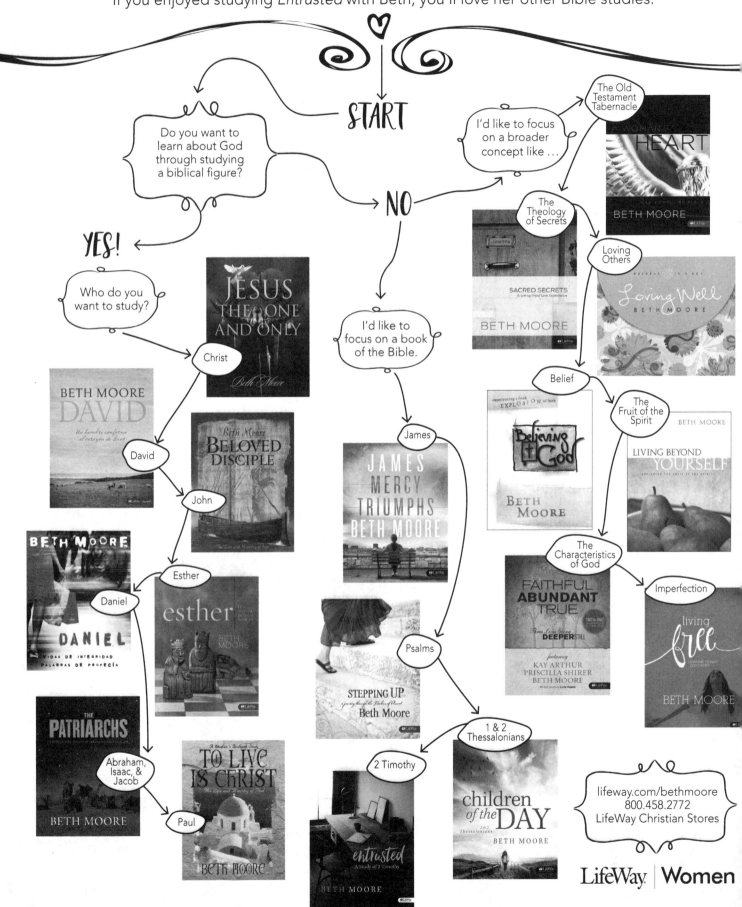

START

Do you want to learn about God through studying a biblical figure?

NO

I'd like to focus on a broader concept like …

The Old Testament Tabernacle

A WOMAN'S HEART
BETH MOORE

YES!

Who do you want to study?

JESUS THE ONE AND ONLY
Beth Moore

Christ

The Theology of Secrets

SACRED SECRETS
A Living Proof Love Experience
BETH MOORE

Loving Others

Loving Well
BETH MOORE

BETH MOORE DAVID
Un hombre conforme al corazón de Dios

David

Beth Moore BELOVED DISCIPLE
The Life and Ministry of John

John

I'd like to focus on a book of the Bible.

James

JAMES MERCY TRIUMPHS BETH MOORE

Belief

EXPLOSION of faith
Believing God
BETH MOORE

The Fruit of the Spirit

BETH MOORE
LIVING BEYOND YOURSELF
Exploring the Fruit of the Spirit

BETH MOORE

Esther

esther
BETH MOORE

DANIEL
VIDAS DE INTEGRIDAD PALABRAS DE PROFECÍA

Daniel

Psalms

STEPPING UP
a journey through the Psalms of Ascent
Beth Moore

The Characteristics of God

FAITHFUL ABUNDANT TRUE
Three Lives Going DEEPER STILL
featuring
KAY ARTHUR
PRISCILLA SHIRER
BETH MOORE

Imperfection

living free
LEARNING TO LIVE IN GOD'S GRACE
BETH MOORE

THE PATRIARCHS

Abraham, Isaac, & Jacob

TO LIVE IS CHRIST
The Life and Ministry of Paul
BETH MOORE

Paul

2 Timothy

1 & 2 Thessalonians

children of the DAY
1&2 Thessalonians
BETH MOORE

entrusted
A Study of 2 Timothy
BETH MOORE

lifeway.com/bethmoore
800.458.2772
LifeWay Christian Stores

LifeWay | Women

CHALLENGE GIRLS TO LIVE AS WORTHY VESSELS OF THE GOSPEL OF JESUS CHRIST.

Worthy Vessel is a six-session resource by Amy Byrd that will lead girls through an in-depth study of 2 Timothy. They will examine biblical context and a multitude of spiritual truths in this letter from the apostle Paul to Timothy. As they explore the relationship between Paul and his young disciple, girls will be challenged to live as worthy vessels of the gospel of Jesus Christ, encouraging others to walk in faith as they deliver the message God has entrusted to them.

AVAILABLE AT LIFEWAY.COM/GIRLS OR AT YOUR LOCAL LIFEWAY CHRISTIAN STORE.

Don't miss a moment of
BETH!

Sign up for the LifeWay Women newsletter to get the latest updates on Beth Moore products, events, giveaways, and more.

lifeway.com/womensnews

LifeWay | Women